CH

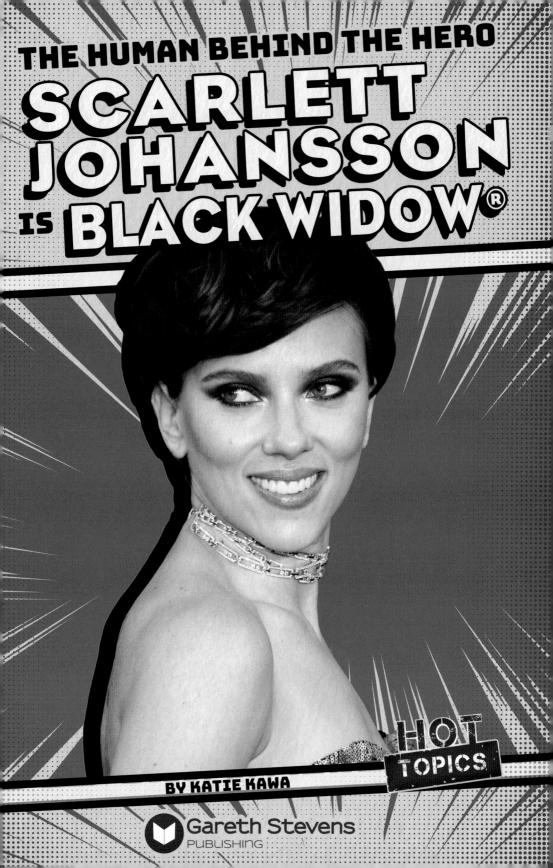

THE HUMAN BEHIND THE HERO

# SCARLETT JOHANSSON

# IS BLACK WIDOW®

HOT TOPICS

BY KATIE KAWA

Gareth Stevens
PUBLISHING

Please visit our website, www.garethstevens.com. For a free color catalog of all our high-quality books, call toll free 1-800-542-2595 or fax 1-877-542-2596.

Cataloging-in-Publication Data

Names: Kawa, Katie.
Title: Scarlett Johansson is Black Widow ®/ Katie Kawa.
Description: New York : Gareth Stevens Publishing, 2020. | Series: The human behind the hero | Includes glossary and index.
Identifiers: ISBN 9781538248355 (pbk.) | ISBN 9781538248379 (library bound) | ISBN 9781538248362 (6 pack)
Subjects: LCSH: Johansson, Scarlett, 1984–Juvenile literature. | Motion picture actors and actresses–United States–Biography–Juvenile literature.
Classification: LCC PN2287.J575 K39 2020 | DDC 791.4302'8092 B–dc23

First Edition

Published in 2020 by
Gareth Stevens Publishing
111 East 14th Street, Suite 349
New York, NY 10003

Designer: Sarah Liddell
Editor: Katie Kawa

Photo credits: Cover, pp. 1, 19 Tinseltown/Shutterstock.com; halftone texture used throughout gn8/Shutterstock.com; comic frame used throughout KID_A/Shutterstock.com; p. 5 Joe Seer/Shutterstock.com; p. 7 Rena Schild/Shutterstock.com; p. 9 Mike Marsland/Contributor/WireImage/Getty Images; p. 11 s_bukley/Shutterstock.com; p. 13 David M. Benett/Shutterstock.com; p. 15 Karwai Tang/Contributor/WireImage/Getty Images; p. 17 Alberto E. Rodriguez/Staff/Getty Images Entertainment/Getty Images; p. 21 Ian West - PA Images/Contributor/PA Images/Getty Images; p. 23 Samir Hussein/Contributor/Getty Images Entertainment/Getty Images; p. 25 Noam Galai/Contributor/WireImage/Getty Images; p. 27 John Sciulli/Stringer/WireImage/Getty Images; p. 29 Rich Polk/Stringer/Getty Images Entertainment/Getty Images.

Printed in the United States of America

Some of the images in this book illustrate individuals who are models. The depictions do not imply actual situations or events.

CPSIA compliance information: Batch #CW20GS: For further information contact Gareth Stevens, New York, New York at 1-800-542-2595.

# CONTENTS

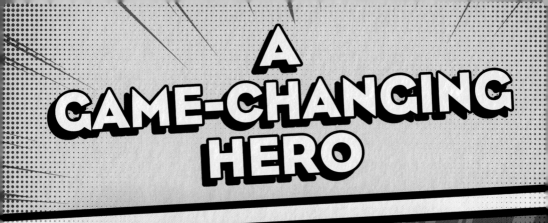

# A GAME-CHANGING HERO

The Avengers are known as "Earth's mightiest heroes." When they came together in their first movie, one woman—Black Widow—was part of this group. By bringing Black Widow to life, Scarlett Johansson helped change the game for women in superhero movies!

## BEHIND THE SCENES

BLACK WIDOW FIRST APPEARED IN MARVEL COMIC BOOKS IN 1964. IN THE COMIC BOOKS, SHE WAS A RUSSIAN SPY WHOSE REAL NAME IS NATALIA ROMANOVA. HOWEVER, SHE'S MORE COMMONLY KNOWN AS NATASHA ROMANOFF.

# A YOUNG ACTRESS

Scarlett Johansson was born on November 22, 1984. She grew up in New York City, and she wanted to be an actress from a young age. In 1994, she got her first part in a movie, which was called *North*.

HUNTER JOHÄNSSON

# BEHIND THE SCENES

SCARLETT HAS A TWIN BROTHER NAMED HUNTER. HE ACTED WITH HER IN THE 1996 MOVIE *MANNY & LO*, BUT HE'S NOT AN ACTOR ANYMORE. HE ONCE WORKED FOR PRESIDENT BARACK OBAMA!

# RISING STAR

Many people first noticed Scarlett's talent in the 1998 movie *The Horse Whisperer*. Then, in 2003, she became even more famous after starring in *Lost in Translation* and *Girl with a Pearl Earring*. Scarlett won **awards** for acting in both of those movies.

# BEHIND THE SCENES

SCARLETT WENT TO SCHOOL AT THE PROFESSIONAL CHILDREN'S SCHOOL IN NEW YORK CITY. THIS IS A SPECIAL SCHOOL FOR YOUNG PEOPLE WHO ARE ALSO WORKING IN MUSIC, MOVIES, DANCE, AND OTHER FIELDS.

9

# BLACK WIDOW'S FIRST MOVIE

In 2010, Scarlett appeared as Black Widow for the first time in the movie *Iron Man 2*. Robert Downey Jr. played Iron Man, who's also known as Tony Stark. Scarlett and Robert became friends during their time working on Marvel movies together.

## BEHIND THE SCENES

THE FIRST CHOICE TO PLAY BLACK WIDOW WAS EMILY BLUNT, WHO'S STARRED IN MOVIES SUCH AS *MARY POPPINS RETURNS*. WHEN SHE HAD TO DROP OUT, SCARLETT WAS CHOSEN TO TAKE HER PLACE IN 2009.

11

# AVENGERS, ASSEMBLE!

Scarlett's next appearance in a Marvel movie was in *The Avengers* in 2012. Black Widow played a big part in this movie and helped bring all the Avengers together. The movie was a huge hit and made more than $1.5 billion around the world!

# BEHIND THE SCENES

SOME PEOPLE CALL THE SIX HEROES WHO STARRED IN *THE AVENGERS* THE "ORIGINAL SIX." THEY'RE HAWKEYE, BLACK WIDOW, THE HULK, THOR, CAPTAIN AMERICA, AND IRON MAN.

# WORKING WITH CAPTAIN AMERICA

Scarlett then played Black Widow in *Captain America: The Winter Soldier*. In this movie, she shared many scenes with Chris Evans, who played Captain America. Scarlett and Chris are good friends who knew each other long before they joined the **Marvel Cinematic Universe**!

CHRIS EVANS

# BEHIND THE SCENES

CAPTAIN AMERICA: THE WINTER SOLDIER CAME OUT IN 2014. THAT SAME YEAR, SCARLETT BECAME A MOM FOR THE FIRST TIME WHEN HER DAUGHTER ROSE WAS BORN.

15

# FROM FRIENDSHIP TO FIGHTING

Marvel kept Scarlett busy! She joined the other Avengers again in 2015's *Avengers: Age of Ultron*. Then, in 2016, she also played Black Widow in *Captain America: Civil War*. In this movie, she had to fight against some of the other Avengers.

## BEHIND THE SCENES

SCARLETT'S VOICE HAS BEEN USED IN MANY MOVIES, INCLUDING *SING* AND *THE JUNGLE BOOK* IN 2016 AND *ISLE OF DOGS* IN 2018. IT WAS ALSO USED IN THE 2013 MOVIE *HER*.

# INFINITY WAR

Scarlett's next Marvel movie—*Avengers: Infinity War*—was one of the most successful superhero movies ever! It made more than $2 billion in ticket sales around the world. Its ending was so shocking that fans couldn't wait to see what Marvel did next.

## BEHIND THE SCENES

SCARLETT'S WORK AS BLACK WIDOW HELPED MAKE HER THE HIGHEST-PAID ACTRESS OF 2018. THAT YEAR, SHE MADE $40.5 MILLION!

# REACHING THE ENDGAME

*Avengers: Endgame* opened in April 2019. It continued the story of *Infinity War* and dealt mainly with the original six Avengers, including Black Widow. This movie was even more successful than *Infinity War*. It made more than $1.2 billion just in its opening weekend!

## BEHIND THE SCENES

WHEN *INFINITY WAR* OPENED, IT SET THE WORLD RECORD FOR THE MOST MONEY MADE IN A MOVIE'S OPENING WEEKEND. A YEAR LATER, *ENDGAME* BROKE THAT RECORD.

# TRAINING LIKE A SUPERHERO

Black Widow is a great fighter, so Scarlett had to train to fight like a superhero. She worked out at least four days a week to be as strong as possible for *Infinity War* and *Endgame*. She lifted weights and did many other exercises too.

# BEHIND THE SCENES

SCARLETT HAS DONE MANY OF HER OWN STUNTS IN HER MOVIES. THESE SPECIAL SKILLS AND TRICKS, SUCH AS JUMPING FROM HIGH PLACES, OFTEN TAKE A LOT OF HARD WORK TO GET RIGHT.

23

# USING HER VOICE

Scarlett is strong in other ways too. She stands up for what she believes in and uses her voice to speak out about causes she cares about, including women's health. She's also spoken at marches about the importance of treating women with respect.

WOMEN'S MARCH
-ON WASHINGTON-

## BEHIND THE SCENES

BY THE TIME *ENDGAME* OPENED, SCARLETT WASN'T THE ONLY **FEMALE MARVEL HERO** ANYMORE. THIS MOVIE HAD A POWERFUL MOMENT WHEN MANY FEMALE HEROES, INCLUDING CAPTAIN MARVEL, THE WASP, AND GAMORA, WORKED TOGETHER.

# BLACK WIDOW'S FUTURE

Many women are **inspired** by Black Widow and see parts of themselves in her story. Scarlett knew it was important to continue telling her story even after *Endgame*. In 2018, it was **announced** that she would be starring in her own movie about Black Widow.

## BEHIND THE SCENES

SCARLETT HAS ACTED IN PLAYS TOO. IN 2010, SHE WAS IN THE PLAY *A VIEW FROM THE BRIDGE* AND WON A TONY AWARD, WHICH IS A FAMOUS AWARD GIVEN FOR ACTING IN A PLAY.

# A POWERFUL WOMAN

Today, there are many powerful women fighting alongside men in superhero movies. Scarlett Johansson's success as Black Widow helped make this possible. By playing the first female Avenger, she's helped many women believe they can be heroes too!

# BEHIND THE SCENES

SCARLETT IS ALSO A SINGER. IN 2008, SHE PUT OUT AN ALBUM CALLED *ANYWHERE I LAY MY HEAD*. THE NEXT YEAR, SHE AND **MUSICIAN** PETE YORN SANG SONGS TOGETHER ON THE ALBUM *BREAK UP*.

# TIMELINE

1984   SCARLETT IS BORN ON NOVEMBER 22.

1994   SCARLETT ACTS IN *NORTH*, WHICH IS HER FIRST MOVIE.

2003   SCARLETT STARS IN *LOST IN TRANSLATION* AND *GIRL WITH A PEARL EARRING*.

2009   SCARLETT IS CHOSEN TO PLAY BLACK WIDOW.

2010   SCARLETT APPEARS AS BLACK WIDOW FOR THE FIRST TIME IN *IRON MAN 2*.

SCARLETT WINS A TONY AWARD FOR *A VIEW FROM THE BRIDGE*.

2012   *THE AVENGERS* OPENS.

2014   SCARLETT STARS WITH CHRIS EVANS IN *CAPTAIN AMERICA: THE WINTER SOLDIER*.

SCARLETT'S DAUGHTER ROSE IS BORN.

2015   *AVENGERS: AGE OF ULTRON* OPENS.

2016   SCARLETT ACTS IN *CAPTAIN AMERICA: CIVIL WAR*.

SCARLETT'S VOICE IS USED IN *THE JUNGLE BOOK* AND *SING*.

2018   *AVENGERS: INFINITY WAR* OPENS.

PLANS FOR A BLACK WIDOW MOVIE ARE ANNOUNCED.

SCARLETT IS NAMED THE YEAR'S HIGHEST-PAID ACTRESS.

2019   SCARLETT PLAYS BLACK WIDOW IN *AVENGERS: ENDGAME*.

# FOR MORE INFORMATION

## BOOKS

Cink, Lorraine. *Powers of a Girl: 65 Marvel Women Who Punched the Sky & Changed the Universe*. Los Angeles, CA: Marvel, 2019.

Delmar, Pete. *Scarlett Johansson*. North Mankato, MN: Capstone Press, 2017.

Dougall, Alastair. *Marvel Avengers: The Greatest Heroes*. London, England: DK, 2018.

## WEBSITES

### IMDb: Scarlett Johansson
*www.imdb.com/name/nm0424060/*
The Internet Movie Database has facts for fans about Scarlett's movies and life.

### Marvel: Black Widow
*www.marvel.com/characters/black-widow-natasha-romanoff*
Visitors to the official Marvel website can learn more about Black Widow in Marvel movies and comic books.

### Marvel HQ
*www.marvelhq.com*
This website is a great place to learn more about Marvel characters through videos, fun facts, and activities.

# GLOSSARY

**announce:** to officially tell people about something

**award:** an honor given for doing something well

**female:** dealing with women or girls

**inspire:** to cause someone to want to do something great

**Marvel Cinematic Universe:** the group of Marvel movies and TV shows that share many of the same characters and began with *Iron Man* in 2008

**musician:** one who plays, makes, or sings music

**original:** first or earliest

# INDEX